#INMYHEALING
EROTIC AFFIRMATIONS JOURNAL

#InMyHealing Erotic Affirmations Journal
Celebrate Your Erotic Self with Pleasure-Affirming Healing Words of Power for Your Mind, Body, Energy, & Spirit

All rights reserved. No part of this book may be reproduced by any mechanical, photographic, or electronic process, or in the form of a phonographic recording; nor may it be stored in a retrieval system, transmitted or otherwise be copied for public or private use, other than "fair use" as brief quotations embodied in articles and reviews without prior written permission of the publisher.

#InMyHealing Erotic Affirmations Journal and SHIFT, A Self-Liberation Healing Practice is not a replacement for professional medical advice and/or psychotherapy. Always consult with a medical physician. Any use of information in this book is at the reader's discretion and risk. Neither the author nor the publisher can be held responsible for any loss, claim, or damage arising out of the use, or misuse of the suggestions made, the failure to take medical advice, or for any material on third-party websites.

Published by TWSHI Publishing
TWSHI Publishing presents H#InMyHealing Erotic Affirmations Journal
Celebrate Your Erotic Self with Pleasure-Affirming Healing Words of Power for
Your Mind, Body, Energy, & Spirit
Text © Lena C. Queen, LCSW, M.Ed.
The moral rights of the author have been asserted.

Printed in the United States of America
Cover Design: Lena Queen
Cover Photo: Lena Queen
Insert Photo of Author: Lena Queen
End Cover Photo: Lena Queen
Stock Photos: Nappy.co
SHIFT Energy Chart Design: Lena Queen
Stock Photos: Nappy.co
Trade Paper ISBN: 9978-1-7364800-3-8

Thank you for choosing you.

With your permission, allow me to remind you: *You are a lover and you are already WHOLE.*

Regardless of "the defaults" of and harmed caused by societal and sexual expectations and assumptions,
our purpose in life is to "live WHOLE pleasurably ".

With this erotic affirmation journal, I give to you some of my most intimate, powerful, and liberated self-reflections. This journal is part of the transformative healing program, Healing The Erotic Self. I give out of the audacity in the hopes that you choose you and to be better for it. That is not to say there won't be a struggle. It is to say have the audacity to center yourself and prioritize yourself the way others have prioritized themselves and become so skilled in your healing-living won't seem like such a struggle and you find was to connect to yourself pleasurably. While this healing work centers the erotic lived experience of Black women, and non-binary folks, this liberatory resource can be applied to all bodies, and all genders.

Self-care is not selfish. Self-care is the act of self-preservation.

Use this journal to discover the healing narrative of your erotic self.

As Ancestor Audre Lorde proclaims:
"Caring for myself is not self-indulgence. It is self-preservation, and that is an act of political warfare."

#INMYHEALING

Lena Queen, LCSW, M.Ed.
LENA QUEEN, LCSW, M.Ed.
Healing The Erotic Self Life
Coaching Program

#INMYHEALING
EROTIC AFFIRMATIONS JOURNAL

TABLE OF CONTENTS

- SEXUAL SHADOW WORK
- USES OF THE EROTIC
- HEALING 101: BECOMING HEALING-CENTERED
- EROTIC AFFIRMATIONS
- PRESENCE PRACTICE: CREATING AN EMPOWERED EMBODIMENT
- SHIFT, A SELF-LIBERATION PRACTICE
- BODY SCAN MEDITATION
- PLEASURE ACTIVISM RESOURCES

Healing the Erotic Self

HealingTheEroticSelf.com

#INMYHEALING
EROTIC AFFIRMATIONS JOURNAL

HEALING 101: BECOMING HEALING-CENTERED

Who are you centering in your healing...?

Healing The Erotic Self fosters your wholisitic relationship to your mind, body, energy, and spirit; its an integrative and somatic relationship. According to Oxford Dictionary-somatic means ""relating to the body, especially m as being distinct from the mind. In western medicine and understanding of embodiment, the mind and body are separate. However, as indigenous medicine and fellow somatic sexologist and founder of Atlanta Tantra Institute, Amina Peterson, reminds us "The body does not exist without the mind." When decolonizing our understanding of somatics, healing, and the erotic, ancestral knowing and neuroscience confirms, the mind and body are part of the wholeness of oneself that includes energy, spirit and intuition. The working of this "parts" to a common understanding of wholeness is integration. Your wholeness or WHOLE-Self is the integration of your emotional, spiritual, sexual, mental, physical, and metaphysical (i.e. energetic) selves.

Healing the Erotic Self is healing the WHOLE-Self.

Healing The Erotic Self Healing System is honoring how your mind, body, spirit, and energy are impacted by both your relationship with yourself and your relationship with others. With uses of the erotic, you will reclaim your power, trust your intuition, and develop a sustainable system of self-care,

#INMYHEALING
EROTIC AFFIRMATIONS JOURNAL

HEALING 101: BECOMING HEALING-CENTERED

Sexual Shadow Work

There is an ancestral and indigenous concept to communities of color (i.e. the global majority) that in western psychology was co-opted by psychiatrist and founder of psychoanalysis Carl Jung used to describe vulnerable parts of one's personality that shows up self-doubt, self-loathing, self-sabotage, self-depreciating, trauma/protective responses, and insecurities. This concept is called "the shadow". While this part of your personality may be part of your unhealed Self that you may not like or be in denial about, your shadow is not always something negative or bad. Self-perception is everything. While the shadow or shadows are known in popular culture for being dark, unwanted, and even evil, I want to disrupt that sentiment. I want to remind you that in the shadow is also where you can rest, grow, find comfort, and protection. When your shadow is informed by your sexual distress, it becomes your sexual shadow.

While healing your shadow requires the engage of your emotional intelligence or the ability to manage and regulate your emotions, healing your sexual shadow will require your emotional intelligence and your erotic intelligence. Erotic intelligence is the ability to be discerning of your desires, sexual and non-sexual, with skills of self-awareness, self-regulation, self-compassion, in addition to, social and relationship awareness, connection, and regulation.

#INMYHEALING
EROTIC AFFIRMATIONS JOURNAL

USES OF THE EROTIC: YOUR HEALING INTENTIONS

In her pleasure manifesto, "Uses of the Erotic", Audre Lorde shares her framework in which self-liberation and community healing is achieved. Uses of the erotic is what Black Funk Studies (Stallings, 2015) calls the "disruption of respectability politics and treatment of the mind, body, and spirit as a unified whole in understanding Black sexuality and gender politics" (p.13). As sexual healing tools,, uses of the erotic honors the self-awareness of the (Black) body (i.e. sensory experience, aesthetics, and embodiment), the (Black) body's relationship to capitalism, Western, and Euro-centric morality, in addition to, the (Black) body labor.

For those with marginalized identities and bodies not Black, it is foundational to also process your relationship to respectability politics which is informed by anti-Blackness racism and it's sexual stereotypes and unpack your relationship to your marginalized and privileged sexuality and gender identity(-ies). This is where therapy or some other coaching and support could help you know more about yourself.

Some of you are here because you have an intuitive understanding that there is more to consider in your lived experience and in your healing by challenging the defaults of societal and sexual expectations and assumptions, The next section explore more about the uses of the erotic as intentions in your healing and how to decolonize the defaults.

#INMYHEALING
EROTIC AFFIRMATIONS JOURNAL

Uses of the Erotic as understood by Audre Lorde

Within her book, Sister Outsider, the pleasure manifesto, Uses of the Erotic, Audre Lorde shares a timeless understanding of the erotic and provides an invaluable guide to how to use the erotic as healing intentions at both the individual & relationship level.

Uses of the erotic requires and allows for what Black Funk Studies calls the "disruption of respectability politics and treatment of the mind, body, and spirit as a unified whole in understanding Black sexuality and gender politics" (Stallings, p.13).

The Seven Uses of the Erotic to use as healing intentions are:
1) Joy
2) Pleasure
3) Sensuality as self-care
4) Acting without self-doubt or shame
5) The reciprocity of emotional labor
6) Vulnerability
7) The Whole Self is the Erotic Self

Reflection Question: How do you currently incorporate the erotic in your healing practices?

_____
_____
_____
_____
_____
_____
_____

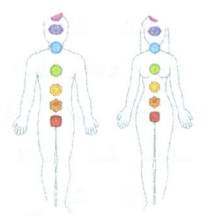

#INMYHEALING
EROTIC AFFIRMATIONS JOURNAL

HEALING 101: BECOMING HEALING-CENTERED

As a trauma-responsive therapist, clinical somatic sexologist, a self-liberator of complex trauma, I am actively engaged in the healing of my erotic self and living fully in that power. As a result, I have learned how to create a system of self-care that supports the effort to unlearn societal defaults about sexuality and somatics, how to manage & and dissolve my sexual distress. This has happened because I develop self-trust and listen to my intuition or my inner knowing to lean into joy and pleasure while (re-)connecting to my mind, body, spirit, and energy. both sexually and non-sexually.

The first step to this self-liberation was moving from my trauma narrative to my healing narrative.

I have learned how to develop an internal dialogue of my radical self-acceptance and radical self-love with erotic affirmations. These words of power center my knowing, my voice, my boundaries, my desires, my needs, and my embodiment in ways that honors both the sexual and the spiritual or energetic parts of my authentic self. It is with these affirmations and my self-liberation practice that I have created a pathway to sustain my self-liberation and my erotic embodiment.

What is healing?

Healing is the return to balanced regulation and feeling of wholeness of one's emotional, mental, spiritual, sexual, physical, and metaphysical selves. As mentioned earlier, healing does not mean the absence of pain nor discomfort. However, healing is an integrative understanding of oneself. This understanding is from a discerning embodiment of wholeness with relationship to your connection to Self and to others.

#INMYHEALING
EROTIC AFFIRMATIONS JOURNAL

Healing is both/and, not either/or.

We have been socialized to accept that shame is the default of our experiences and pleasure requires sacrifice. For that reason, we often think that healing is about choosing instead of *accepting* that complex truths can hold the same place. This is because acceptance requires empathy and compassion. However, empathy and compassion does not fit in the narrative of shame.

Self-Compassion: How are you holding space for yourself?

Healing is not about staying peaceful, it's about being able to and the capacity to return to peace. What I like to call-controlled chaos. Depression, anxiety, self-doubt, self-worth, self-confidence are all impacted by our everyday living. The "magic", if you will that requires you to activate self-permission (i.e. your power) to engage in your healing is -self-compassion. The care, concern, ad understanding you give others- I challenge you to give yourself.

Being healing-centered means we are centering our ability to pour into ourselves without shame or guilt. Holding space is a liberatory practice from the U.S. Healing Justice Movement.

Healing Justice (2010) is a term coined by disabled Southern (U.S.) Black & Native femmes, healers, and reproductive justice movement leaders to honor the historical communal connections within justice movements and the need for movement spaces to address the mental, emotional, spiritual, and physical burnout and complex trauma movement activists, communities of color, and marginalized bodies experience. Holding Space is a practice of being present with intention to be empathetic for another human being, or in this case, for yourself.

> "Our movements themselves have to be healing, or there's no point to them."
> —Cara Page, Kindred: Southern Healing JusticeCollective

#INMYHEALING
EROTIC AFFIRMATIONS JOURNAL
HEALING 101: BECOMING HEALING-CENTERED

What we know about desire has usually been taught to us. We have been told that erotic is sexual only. However, the erotic is not just sexual because desire is not just sexual. The erotic is the energy of desirability, both sexual and non-sexual. And from that teaching of desire, we have also been taught what is respectable, what is successful, what has influence or social capital, and what has value. We have been taught to reach for someone's dreams and expectations for us- for another's desires, not our own. By engaging in sexual shadow work, you reclaim your embodied power to be in a consensual and safer relationship with both your body and your desires.

Erotic intelligence is the intuitive and discerning ability to navigate love, desire, intimacy, and your erotic power with authenticity and erotic curiosity in your everyday live, The purpose of this journal is to support you in developing an erotically affirming internal dialogue as you create your healing narrative; your story from the center of your desires and your power.

#INMYHEALING
EROTIC AFFIRMATIONS JOURNAL

REFLECTION ACTIVITY: Set your intentions with how you will use this self reflection journal to create an empowering erotic mindset. Take a deep breath. Relax your shoulders and lean into this reflection activity. Answer the reflections below.

REFLECTION #1: What was your goal(s) using this journal?

REFLECTION #2: What do you think could be a challenge your meeting these intentions?

REFLECTION #3: How will you know if you have made any progress in achieving your intentions?

I am Grounded

To be grounded is to root myself in the present moment, deeply connected to my wholeness and the earth beneath me. Being grounded reminds me that my erotic energy is most powerful when anchored in self-awareness and stability. My groundedness allows my desires to flourish naturally, creating a foundation for pleasure, safety, and self-trust.

EROTIC AFFIRMATIONS
#InMyHealing
IG:@HealingTheEroticSelf

#INMYHEALING
EROTIC AFFIRMATIONS JOURNAL

I AM GROUNDED

HEALING PRACTICE:
USE THIS AFFIRMATION AS INTENTION IN YOUR PRESENCE PRACTICE RELATED TO YOUR ABILITY TO WITNESS YOURSELF WITHOUT JUDGEMENT.

REFLECTIONS: WHAT IS YOUR RELATIONSHIP TO SELF-COMPASSION & SELF-ACCEPTANCE?

JOURNAL YOUR REFLECTIONS BELOW.

_____
_____
_____
_____
_____
_____
_____
_____
_____
_____
_____
_____
_____
_____

DID YOU KNOW THE HUMAN BODY, YOUR BODY, HAS ENERGY PORTALS LOCATED ALONG THE SPINE WITHIN OUR ENDOCRINE GLANDS OR HORMONAL SYSTEM? THIS ENERGY SYSTEM IS KNOWN AS CHAKRA (HINDI SYSTEM) AND ARIT/ARITU (KEMETIC SYSTEM).

I am Centered

To be centered is to return to myself, grounding deeply in the core of who I am. I embrace my erotic energy as an anchor to keep me centered & allow my desires flow with clarity and intention, unshaken by outside noise or expectations. My wholeness becomes a sacred compass, guiding me toward what feels right and true. With this my sensuality blossoms—not as something I seek but as something I embody. Centered and whole, I radiate confidence and calm, drawing strength from the deep well of my erotic self.

Erotic Affirmations Journal
#INMYHEALING
@HealingTheEroticSelf

#INMYHEALING
EROTIC AFFIRMATIONS JOURNAL

I AM CENTERED

HEALING PRACTICE:
WHEN YOU ARE FEELING CONFLICTED IN THE MOMENT OF CHOOSING YOURSELF,

ASK YOURSELF:
(1) WHAT IS IN MY BEST INTEREST?
(2) IN THIS MOMENT, WHAT IS THE PURPOSE OF MY INTERACTIONS? NAME YOUR INTENTION.
(3) IN THIS MOMENT WHO AM I CENTERING?

REFLECTIONS: IHOW WILL YOU ALLOW YOUR EROTIC ENERGY TO GUIDE YOU & PRIORTIZE YOUR CHOICES?

JOURNAL YOUR REFLECTIONS BELOW.

___
___
___
___
___
___
___
___
___
___
___
___
___
___

SCIENTIFICALLY, IT HAS BEEN SHOWN THERE IS A RELATIONSHIP BETWEEN YOUR HORMONES, YOUR MOODS, YOUR MINDSET, AND YOUR MOVEMENTS (DECISION-MAKING AND BEHAVIORS).

I am Nurtured

I know my relationship to my senses and how to self-soothe. I will intentionally take care of myself with a healing practice in relationship to all of my senses. My healing practice protects & encourages my growth, my strength, & my transformation.

Erotic Affirmations Journal
#INMYHEALING

@HealingTheEroticSelf

#INMYHEALING
EROTIC AFFIRMATIONS JOURNAL

I AM NURTURED

HEALING PRACTICE:
USE THIS AFFIRMATION AS INTENTION IN YOUR PRESENCE PRACTICE RELATED TO YOUR ABILITY TO PRACTICE INTENTIONAL CARE OF YOUR MIND, BODY, ENERGY, & SPIRIT.

REFLECTIONS: WHAT IS YOUR RELATIONSHIP TO TAKING CARE OF YOURSELF?

JOURNAL YOUR REFLECTIONS BELOW.

___

DID YOU KNOW THERE ARE 7 HORMONAL SYSTEMS IN THE BODY FOR MOST HUMANS? INTERSEX FOLKS MAY HAVE 8 HORMONAL SYSTEMS.

I am Affirmed

I speak life into me. I embodied the healing I have intentionally set to become. My answers come from within. I do not need anyone's permission but my own to be liberated.

Erotic Affirmations Journal
#INMYHEALING

@HealingTheEroticSelf

#INMYHEALING
EROTIC AFFIRMATIONS JOURNAL

I AM AFFIRMED

HEALING PRACTICE:
USE THIS AFFIRMATION AS INTENTION IN YOUR PRESENCE PRACTICE RELATED TO YOUR ABILITY TO ENCOURAGING YOURSELF WHEN YOU ARE STRUGGLING.

REFLECTIONS: WHAT IS YOUR RELATIONSHIP TO YOUR INTERNAL DIALOGUE/SELF-TALK?

JOURNAL YOUR REFLECTIONS BELOW.

_____
_____
_____
_____
_____
_____
_____
_____
_____
_____
_____
_____
_____
_____

EACH HORMONAL CENTER CREATES DIFFERENT ENERGY FREQUENCIES COMMONLY KNOWN AS HEALING THEMES OF THE BODY'S ENERGY CENTERS.

I am Intentional

I choose to be purposeful in this moment. I will be mindful of how much energy and care I put into things that serve me. For my healing, I will protect myself until I can release what no longer serves me.

Erotic Affirmations Journal
#INMYHEALING

@HealingThe EroticSelf

#INMYHEALING
EROTIC AFFIRMATIONS JOURNAL

I AM INTENTIONAL

HEALING PRACTICE:
USE THIS AFFIRMATION AS INTENTION IN YOUR PRESENCE PRACTICE RELATED TO YOUR ABILITY TO BEING PURPOSEFULLY IN THE PRESENT MOMENT.

REFLECTIONS: WHAT IS YOUR RELATIONSHIP TO YOUR COMMITMENT TO YOURSELF?

JOURNAL YOUR REFLECTIONS BELOW.

_____
_____
_____
_____
_____
_____
_____
_____
_____
_____
_____
_____
_____
_____

THE 1ST ENERGY CENTER IS LOCATED IN THE BOTTOM OF YOUR REPRODUCTIVE GLANDS. THE HEALING THEME OF THIS ENERGY CENTER IS SAFETY AND STABILITY.

I am Present

I am attentive in this moment of time, energy, and space. I am connected to my ability to keep myself safe- mind, body, & spirit. No multi-tasking, no searching.

I only need to focus and do things one action at a time.

Erotic Affirmations Journal
#INMYHEALING

@HealingThe EroticSelf

#INMYHEALING
EROTIC AFFIRMATIONS JOURNAL

I AM PRESENT

HEALING PRACTICE:
USE THIS AFFIRMATION AS INTENTION IN YOUR PRESENCE PRACTICE RELATED TO YOUR ABILITY TO BEING IN THE "HERE AND NOW".

REFLECTIONS: WHAT IS YOUR RELATIONSHIP TO BEING PRESENT IN THE CURRENT MOMENT?

JOURNAL YOUR REFLECTIONS BELOW.

_____
_____
_____
_____
_____
_____
_____
_____
_____
_____
_____
_____
_____

THE 2ND ENERGY CENTER IS LOCATED BETWEEN THE TOP OF YOUR REPRODUCTIVE GLANDS & YOUR ADRENAL GLANDS. THE HEALING THEME OF THIS ENERGY CENTER IS CREATIVITY & DESIRABILITY, BOTH SEXUAL AND NON-SEXUAL.

I am Intuitive

I trust my relationship to my energy, my spirit, and my inner self. My inner voice guides me with the wisdom of that trust and my connection to my truth.

I am intuitive & not in fear of my authentic self.

Erotic Affirmations Journal
#INMYHEALING
@HealingThe EroticSelf

#INMYHEALING
EROTIC AFFIRMATIONS JOURNAL

I AM INTUTITIVE

HEALING PRACTICE:
USE THIS AFFIRMATION AS INTENTION IN YOUR PRESENCE PRACTICE RELATED TO YOUR ABILITY TO TRUST YOURSELF.

REFLECTIONS: WHAT IS YOUR RELATIONSHIP TO SELF-TRUST?

JOURNAL YOUR REFLECTIONS BELOW.

___

YOUR BODY'S NERVOUS SYSTEM CREATES ELECTRICAL IMPLUSES. WHEN THESE IMPLUSES INTERACT WITH THE ENERGY OF OUR MOODS, THEY BECOME OUR EMOTIONS. JUST LIKE ELECTRICITY, OUR EMOTIONS IS MEASURED IN FREQUENCY.

I am Gentle with myself.

I treat myself with compassion and grace. I engage my senses with the deliberate desirability. The care and concern I give myself is the standard. I give myself permission to be self-accountable with compassion.

I lean into the warmth and comfort of self-desirability.

Erotic Affirmations Journal
#INMYHEALING

@HealingThe EroticSelf

#INMYHEALING
EROTIC AFFIRMATIONS JOURNAL

I AM GENTLE WITH MYSELF

HEALING PRACTICE:
USE THIS AFFIRMATION AS INTENTION IN YOUR PRESENCE PRACTICE RELATED TO YOUR ABILITY TO BE KIND TO YOURSELF.

REFLECTIONS: WHAT IS YOUR RELATIONSHIP WITH SELF-COMPASSION?

JOURNAL YOUR REFLECTIONS BELOW.

_____
_____
_____
_____
_____
_____
_____
_____
_____
_____
_____
_____
_____
_____

THE 3RD CENTER IS LOCATED. 3 FINGERS ABOVE THE BELLY BUTTON IN THE AREAS OF YOUR STOMACH AND YOUR PANCREAS. THE HEALING THEMES'S OF THE THIRD ENERGY CENTER IS CONNECTION WITH OTHERS, SELF-CONFIDENCE, AND PERCEPTION. ONE PART OF YOUR INTUITION "THAT GUT FEELING".

I am Self-Aware

My relationship to my touch, my senses, my emotions, my body, my pleasure, my desirability, and my spirit is known to me. I know what I know about myself. My healing increases the intimacy between me, myself, and I. That intimacy is my lovership, a commitment to knowing I am self-love and fulfillment it brings.

I am self-aware.

Erotic Affirmations Journal
#INMYHEALING
@HealingTheEroticSelf

#INMYHEALING
EROTIC AFFIRMATIONS JOURNAL

I AM SELF-AWARE

HEALING PRACTICE:
USE THIS AFFIRMATION AS INTENTION IN YOUR PRESENCE PRACTICE RELATED TO YOUR ABILITY TO HONOR YOURSELF AND WHAT YOU ARE EXPERIENCING.

REFLECTIONS: WHAT IS YOUR RELATIONSHIP TO SELF-LOVE?

JOURNAL YOUR REFLECTIONS BELOW.

_____
_____
_____
_____
_____
_____
_____
_____
_____
_____
_____
_____
_____

THE 4TH ENERGY CENTER IS LOCATED IN YOUR HEART & THUMUS.
THE HEALING THEME OF THIS CENTER IS SELF-LOVE, LOVE, SELF-COMPASSION, EMPATHY, HOPE, & OPTIMISIM.

I am Desirable

I have discovered myself. Through the journey of exploration of my core desires, I have learned my turn-ons and turn-offs. I am exercising my power to choose experiences of pleasure, people, and relationships that delight MY senses...my desirability. My desirability radiates from my confidence, authenticity, and unapologetic self-expression. My desirability is a reflection of my love for yourself, a testament to the beauty of my erotic and vibrant self.

Erotic Affirmations Journal
#INMYHEALING

@HealingThe EroticSelf

#INMYHEALING
EROTIC AFFIRMATIONS JOURNAL

I AM DESIRABLE

HEALING PRACTICE:
USE THIS AFFIRMATION AS INTENTION IN YOUR PRESENCE PRACTICERELATED TO YOUR ABILITY TO TAP INTO FEELING SEXY AND ATTRACT TO YOURSELF.

REFLECTIONS: WHAT IS YOUR RELATIONSHIP TO FEELING SEXY AND DESIRABLE?

JOURNAL YOUR REFLECTIONS BELOW.

THE 5TH ENERGY CENTER IS LOCATED IN YOUR THROAT WHERE YOUR THRIOD IS.
THE HEALING THEMES OF THIS CENTER IS TRUTH & COMMUNICATION.

I am Sensual

My connection to pleasure engages me to the delight of my senses. That connection reminds me that my senses are both spiritual and sexual. I reclaim my power from oppressive messages about my embodiment. I honor the messages and warnings from my senses. Deep breath in, cool air moves gently into my chest. I notice the expansion of my chest. The music of my breath & the power of my command.
I remember- I am sensual.

Erotic Affirmations Journal
#INMYHEALING

@HealingTheEroticSelf

#INMYHEALING
EROTIC AFFIRMATIONS JOURNAL

I AM SENSUAL

HEALING PRACTICE:
USE THIS AFFIRMATION AS INTENTION IN YOUR PRESENCE PRACTICE RELATED TO YOUR ABILITY TO EXPERIENCE PLEASURE.

REFLECTIONS: WHAT IS YOUR RELATIONSHIP TO YOUR SENSES-TOUCH, TASTE, SIGHT, SMELL, AND HEARING?

JOURNAL YOUR REFLECTIONS BELOW.

_____
_____
_____
_____
_____
_____
_____
_____
_____
_____
_____
_____
_____
_____

YOUR THOUGHTS AND YOUR EMOTIONS CREATE YOUR MINDSET. CHANGE YOUR MINDSET. CHANGE YOUR LIFE.

I am Abundant

Abundance comes from within. It is not reflection of my circumstance, it is a reflection of my outlook, my point of view, my perception. An abundance mindset requires me to challenge what I have been taught has value & to create my own understanding of value.

Abundance is rooted in my sense of value, outside of my labor to others.

Erotic Affirmations Journal
#INMYHEALING
@HealingThe EroticSelf

#INMYHEALING
EROTIC AFFIRMATIONS JOURNAL

I AM ABUNDANT

HEALING PRACTICE:
USE THIS AFFIRMATION AS INTENTION IN YOUR PRESENCE PRACTICE RELATED TO YOUR ABILITY TO YOUR SELF-WORTH.

REFLECTIONS: WHAT IS YOUR RELATIONSHIP TO SELF-WORTH AND YOUR LABOR TO OTHERS?

JOURNAL YOUR REFLECTIONS BELOW.

_____
_____
_____
_____
_____
_____
_____
_____
_____
_____
_____
_____
_____
_____
_____

HEALING ARTS LIKE MEDITATION, BREATHWORK, SELF-REIKI, AND GENTLE MOVEMENTS LIKE STRETCHING, & YOGA CAN CHANGE THE FREQUENCY OF YOUR EMOTIONS OVER TIME. THESE PRACTICES HAVE BEEN CLINICALLY SHOWN TO IMPROVE ANXIETY, DEPRESSION, AND POST-TRAUMATIC STRESS SYMPTOMS.

I am Erotic

I am my BEST lover. I embody the power to create with my lovership. I give my self permission to explore my touch, my taste, my pleasure intertwining with MY Divine erotic energy. I find delight in my growth as I let go of the desires that no longer serve me. And with embodied safety and intuitive self-trust, I find pleasure in the becoming of me.

I am erotic.

Erotic Affirmations Journal
#INMYHEALING

@HealingThe EroticSelf

#INMYHEALING
EROTIC AFFIRMATIONS JOURNAL

I AM EROTIC

HEALING PRACTICE:
USE THIS AFFIRMATION AS INTENTION IN YOUR PRESENCE PRACTICE RELATED TO YOUR ABILITY TO YOUR EROTIC ENERGY.

REFLECTIONS: WHAT IS YOUR RELATIONSHIP TO THE ENERGY OF YOUR SELF-ESTEEM?

JOURNAL YOUR REFLECTIONS BELOW.

_____
_____
_____
_____
_____
_____
_____
_____
_____
_____
_____
_____
_____
_____
_____

YOUR 6TH ENERGY CENTER IS LOCATED BETWEEN YOUR BROWS. THIS IS WHERE THE PITUATRY AND HYPOTHALMUS GLANDS ARE LOCATED. THE HEALING THEME OF THIS CENTER IS SELF-AWARENESS, SELF-ESTEEM, AND DISCERNMENT. THE 2ND HALF OF YOUR INTUITION.

I am Fulfilled

My thoughts are my loving affirmations. My body is my sacred space. My spirit is my Divinity. My joy is my pleasure. My shadow is my most tender and vulnerable self and deserves healing and protection. My desires is my erotic energy. My knowing my Self is my Power and that fulfills me.

Erotic Affirmations Journal
#INMYHEALING
@HealingTheEroticSelf

#INMYHEALING
EROTIC AFFIRMATIONS JOURNAL
I AM FULFILLED

HEALING PRACTICE:
USE THIS AFFIRMATION AS INTENTION IN YOUR PRESENCE PRACTICE RELATED TO YOUR ABILITY TO BE FULFILLED.

REFLECTIONS: WHAT IS YOUR RELATIONSHIP TO KNOWING YOU ARE ENOUGH? JOURNAL YOUR REFLECTIONS BELOW.

_____
_____
_____
_____
_____
_____
_____
_____
_____
_____
_____
_____
_____

ACCORDING TO THE PRACTICE OF NEUROSCIENCE, CREATING AFFIRMATIONS REQUIRES YOU BEING BOTH PRESENT AND INTENTIONAL. YOU MUST KNOW AND BELIEVE IN THE AFFIRMATION TO EMBODY IT. PRACTICING AFFIRMATIONS EACH DAY WILL IMPROVE YOUR ABILITY TO EMBODY WHAT YOU BELIEVE AND WHAT YOU KNOW.

I am Joyful

I believe in my healing. From a place gratitude, I give myself permission to lean wihout shame into my pleasure. I understand soulfully deep pleasure is my birthright.

That pleasure is my joy. I am joyful.

Erotic Affirmations Journal
#INMYHEALING
@HealingThe EroticSelf

#INMYHEALING
EROTIC AFFIRMATIONS JOURNAL

I AM JOYFUL

HEALING PRACTICE:
USE THIS AFFIRMATION AS INTENTION IN YOUR PRESENCE PRACTICE RELATED TO YOUR ABILITY TO CONNECT TO PLEASURE WITHOUT SHAME.

REFLECTIONS: WHAT IS YOUR RELATIONSHIP TO SHAME?

JOURNAL YOUR REFLECTIONS BELOW.

_____
_____
_____
_____
_____
_____
_____
_____
_____
_____
_____
_____
_____
_____

THE 7TH ENERGY IS LOCATED TOWARDS THE TOP BACK OF THE HEAD WHERE THE PINEAL GLAND IS LOCATED. THE HEALING THEME OF THIS GLAND IS KNOWING ONE'S SELF, DIVINITY AND CONNECTION TO SOURCE.

I am Connected

With intentional self-awareness to my relationship with my mind, my body, & my energy, I feel ME. Gently, I remind that I AM the result of my healing. I remind myself that every moment & breath is one I have never taken before. My connection to me is my connection to living.

Erotic Affirmations Journal
#INMYHEALING

@HealingThe EroticSelf

#INMYHEALING
EROTIC AFFIRMATIONS JOURNAL

I AM CONNECTED

HEALING PRACTICE:
USE THIS AFFIRMATION AS INTENTION IN YOUR PRESENCE PRACTICE TO YOUR ABILITY TO KNOW YOU ARE THE FRUIT OF YOUR LABOR.

REFLECTIONS: WHAT IS YOUR RELATIONSHIP TO FEELING EMBODIED?

JOURNAL YOUR REFLECTIONS BELOW.

_____
_____
_____
_____
_____
_____
_____
_____
_____
_____
_____
_____
_____
_____

JUST AS YOUR HORMONAL CENTERS, YOUR HEALING CENTERS WORK IN RELATIONSHIP WITH EACH OTHER.

I am Pleasure

I am the experience of joy, pleasure, and happiness. I am the Divine & the Human Experience feeling connected to my body. I communicate with my senses and feel the desire of my own company. It is with discernment I choose to share my pleasure with.

Erotic Affirmations Journal
#INMYHEALING

@HealingTheEroticSelf

#INMYHEALING
EROTIC AFFIRMATIONS JOURNAL

I AM PLEASURE

HEALING PRACTICE:
USE THIS AFFIRMATION AS INTENTION IN YOUR PRESENCE PRACTICE RELATED TO YOUR ABILITY TO CHOOSE WHAT PLEASES YOU.

REFLECTIONS: WHAT IS YOUR RELATIONSHIP TO SETTING BOUNDARIES?

JOURNAL YOUR REFLECTIONS BELOW.

___

YOU CAN EXPERIENCE PLEASURE IN EACH ENERGY CENTER.

I am Sexy

I own the truth that I am magnetically alluring—an energy that radiates from within. I am alluring in every way—through my presence, my walk, my laughter, my gaze, and my touch. My sensuality is a force that draws others in, but more importantly, it draws me closer to my own desires. I allow myself to bathe in the power of my sexiness, knowing that it's a celebration of who I am, unapologetically and authentically.

Erotic Affirmations Journal
#INMYHEALING

@HealingThe EroticSelf

#INMYHEALING
EROTIC AFFIRMATIONS JOURNAL

I AM SEXY

HEALING PRACTICE:
USE THIS AFFIRMATION AS INTENTION IN YOUR PRESENCE PRACTICE RELATED TO YOUR ABILITY TO BELIEVING IN WHO YOU ARE.

REFLECTIONS: WHAT IS YOUR RELATIONSHIP TO CONFIDENCE?
JOURNAL YOUR REFLECTIONS BELOW.

_____
_____
_____
_____
_____
_____
_____
_____
_____
_____
_____
_____
_____
_____

YOUR LOVERSHIP IS THE PRESENT PRACTICE OF YOUR EROTIC SELF-AWARENESS.

I am Lovable

I have the relationship with myself that I have truly desire. My value & self-worth is determined by no other measuring stick than my own. The safety, joy, affection, & honor I give myself is a direct reflection of my relationship with Self.

I am lovable.

Erotic Affirmations Journal
#INMYHEALING
@HealingThe EroticSelf

#INMYHEALING
EROTIC AFFIRMATIONS JOURNAL

I AM LOVABLE

HEALING PRACTICE:
USE THIS AFFIRMATION AS INTENTION IN YOUR PRESENCE PRACTICE RELATED TO YOUR ABILITY TO LOVE AS AN EXPERIENCE.

REFLECTIONS: WHAT IS YOUR RELATIONSHIP TO LOVE?

JOURNAL YOUR REFLECTIONS BELOW.

_____
_____
_____
_____
_____
_____
_____
_____
_____
_____
_____
_____
_____
_____
_____

LOVE IS NOT JUST AN EMOTION. IT IS AN ACTIONABLE EXPERIENCE. ACCORDING TO BELL HOOKS, LOVE COMPRISES OF SEVEN CHARACTERISTICS. THEY INCLUDE: (1) CARE, (2) AFFECTION, (3) RECOGNITION, (4) RESPECT, (5) COMMITTMENT, (6) TRUST, AND (7) HONEST AND OPEN COMMUNICATION.

I am Divine

I look and I see me. I inhale and I feel me. I smile and I taste me. EYE observe with a knowing of my power. I have the power to create & transform. My power is an extension of my Source, revered & respected. I am Divine.

Erotic Affirmations Journal
#INMYHEALING
@HealingTheEroticSelf

#INMYHEALING
EROTIC AFFIRMATIONS JOURNAL

I AM DIVINE

HEALING PRACTICE:
USE THIS AFFIRMATION AS INTENTION IN YOUR PRESENCE PRACTICE RELATED TO YOUR ABILITY TO YOUR SPIRITUAL SELF.

REFLECTIONS: WHAT IS YOUR RELATIONSHIP TO YOUR SPIRIT?

JOURNAL YOUR REFLECTIONS BELOW.

_____
_____
_____
_____
_____
_____
_____
_____
_____
_____
_____
_____
_____
_____

YOUR SPIRIT IS YOUR CONSCIOUS AWARENESS OF YOUR ENERGY. YOUR SPIRITUALITY IS YOU.R CONNECTION TO A UNIVERSAL SOURCE. OUTSIDE OF RELIGION.

I am Discerning

I trust my intuition & the wisdom that my body holds. Through my erotic energy, I have the ability to navigate my interactions and relationships with certainty. I recognize and honor my value and my values. My insight guides the decisions I make and creates the life & relationships I want for myself.

Erotic Affirmations Journal
#INMYHEALING

@HealingThe EroticSelf

#INMYHEALING
EROTIC AFFIRMATIONS JOURNAL

I AM DISCERNING

HEALING PRACTICE:
USE THIS AFFIRMATION AS INTENTION IN YOUR PRESENCE PRACTICERELATED TO YOUR ABILITY TO JUDGE WELL.

REFLECTIONS: WHAT IS YOUR RELATIONSHIP TO SELF-DOUBT?

JOURNAL YOUR REFLECTIONS BELOW.

___

DISCERNMENT REQUIRES ACCURATE PERCEPTION, SELF-CONFIDENCE, SELF-TRUST, & SELF-AWARENESS.

I am POWER

My erotic energy is power. My power includes my autonomy which is my ability to make decisions and my agency which is my ability to act on the decisions I make. I am capable of exercising my agency & autonomy. I am from within my erotic energy.

I am POWER.

Erotic Affirmations Journal
#INMYHEALING
@HealingThe EroticSelf

#INMYHEALING
EROTIC AFFIRMATIONS JOURNAL

I AM POWER

HEALING PRACTICE:
USE THIS AFFIRMATION AS INTENTION IN YOUR PRESENCE PRACTICE RELATED TO YOUR ABILITY TO MAKE DECISIONS FOR YOURSELF.

REFLECTIONS: WHAT IS YOUR RELATIONSHIP TO REJECTION?

JOURNAL YOUR REFLECTIONS BELOW.

_____
_____
_____
_____
_____
_____
_____
_____
_____
_____
_____
_____
_____
_____

BELIEVE IN YOUR POWER.

I am ENERGY

I am a vessel of dynamic, flowing energy—vibrant, sensual, and alive. This affirmation calls you to recognize your erotic essence as a boundless force that pulses through every aspect of your being. My energy is electric, radiating through my thoughts, movements, and connections, igniting everything I touch. To claim "I am energy" is to honor the infinite power within me—the energy that creates, heals, and desires. I am a luminous, magnetic presence in the world.

I am energy.

Erotic Affirmations Journal
#INMYHEALING
@HealingTheEroticSelf

#INMYHEALING
EROTIC AFFIRMATIONS JOURNAL

I AM ENERGY

HEALING PRACTICE:
USE THIS AFFIRMATION AS INTENTION IN YOUR PRESENCE PRACTICE RELATED TO YOUR ABILITY TO YOUR VULNERABILITY.

REFLECTIONS: WHAT IS YOUR RELATIONSHIP TO BEING EMOTIONALLY AVAILABLE?

JOURNAL YOUR REFLECTIONS BELOW.

_____
_____
_____
_____
_____
_____
_____
_____
_____
_____
_____
_____
_____
_____

BREATHWORK IS CHANGES YOUR ENERGY THAT CAUSES EMOTIONALLY REGULATION.

I am WHOLE

I am my conscious, subconscious, and unconscious perceptions or inner understandings of my mind, body, energy, and spirit. This is embodiment of my emotions, my thoughts, my beliefs that creates my mindset, and informs my behaviors. My embodiment is- also related to my gender, who I am attracted to, in addition to, my relationship to pleasure, pain, power and how I live in your body.

And with this, I understand I am WHOLE. Period. FULL STOP.

Erotic Affirmations Journal
#INMYHEALING

@HealingThe EroticSelf

#INMYHEALING
EROTIC AFFIRMATIONS JOURNAL

I AM WHOLE

HEALING PRACTICE:
USE THIS AFFIRMATION AS INTENTION IN YOUR PRESENCE PRACTICE RELATED TO YOUR ABILITY TO DISRUPT A NEGATIVE SELF-PERCEPTION.

REFLECTIONS: WHAT IS YOUR RELATIONSHIP TO YOUR WHOLENESS, THE FEELING OF BEING WHOLE?

JOURNAL YOUR REFLECTIONS BELOW.

_____
_____
_____
_____
_____
_____
_____
_____
_____
_____
_____
_____
_____
_____
_____

YOUR WHOLENESS IS THE STARTING POINT, NOT THE DESTINTATION. YOU ARE ALREADY WHOLE.

I am Choosing ME

I refuse to self-sacrifice or self-sabotage. It will be "fuck 'em" before its "fuck me" or "fuck it". Choosing myself is an act of radical love, an erotic reclamation of your worth and desires. I am no longer waiting for permission or validation to prioritize my pleasure, boundaries, and joy. I will live with intention courageously. I live with the purpose to be my greatest and most erotic self this lifetime.

Erotic Affirmations Journal
#INMYHEALING
@HealingThe EroticSelf

#INMYHEALING
EROTIC AFFIRMATIONS JOURNAL

I AM CHOOSING ME

HEALING PRACTICE:
USE THIS AFFIRMATION AS INTENTION IN YOUR PRESENCE PRACTICE RELATED TO YOUR ABILITY TO TAKE CARE OF YOUR NEEDS.

REFLECTIONS: WHAT IS YOUR RELATIONSHIP TO FEELING GUILTY WHE SETTING BOUNDARIES?

JOURNAL YOUR REFLECTIONS BELOW.

___

"ONCE YOU KNOW WHO YOU ARE, YOU DON'T HAVE TO WORRY ANYMORE."
-NIKKI GIOVANNI

I am Beautiful

Since beauty is in the eye of the beholder, then I will commit to using my own standards of beauty. I recognize I create beauty and with this visionary power, I chose to see in me what is pleasuring to my EYE.

Therefore, I am beautiful.

Erotic Affirmations Journal
#INMYHEALING

@HealingThe EroticSelf

#INMYHEALING
EROTIC AFFIRMATIONS JOURNAL

I AM BEAUTIFUL

HEALING PRACTICE:
USE THIS AFFIRMATION AS INTENTION IN YOUR PRESENCE PRACTICE RELATED TO YOUR ABILITY TO CREATE WHAT IS PLEASING TO YOU BOTH VISUALLY AND EXPERIENTIALLY.

REFLECTIONS: WHAT IS YOUR RELATIONSHIP TO YOUR BEAUTY?

JOURNAL YOUR REFLECTIONS BELOW.

"THE PRICE WE PAY FOR BEING OURSELVES IS WORTH IT."
-EARTHA KITT

I am a Conquror

I reclaim parts of myself that have been silenced, shamed, or overlooked. You are a conqueror of self-doubt, a vanquisher of shame, and a warrior of pleasure. Each step I take toward owning my erotic energy is an act of triumph over the narratives that once confined me. I stand tall in my sensual authority, knowing that my strength lies not only in enduring but in thriving unapologetically. Through my erotic energy, liberate myself fully.

Erotic Affirmations Journal
#INMYHEALING
@HealingThe EroticSelf

#INMYHEALING
EROTIC AFFIRMATIONS JOURNAL

I AM A CONQUEROR

HEALING PRACTICE:
USE THIS AFFIRMATION AS INTENTION IN YOUR PRESENCE PRACTICE TO LIBERATE YOURSELF.

REFLECTIONS: WHAT IS YOUR RELATIONSHIP TO SELF-LIBERATION?

JOURNAL YOUR REFLECTIONS BELOW.

ONCE YOU GIVE YOURSELF PERMISSION TO BE LIBERATED. YOU STOP WAITING ON ANYONE'S PERMISSION TO BE AUTHENTIC.

I am Embodied

To be embodied is to live fully within the sanctuary of my own being, I embrace the beauty and wisdom of my WHOLE-Self and I will inhabit every sensation, breath, and movement with presence and gratitude. I honor the connection between my mind, body, energy, and spirit, allowing desire and pleasure to flow freely. My embodiment is an act of defiance against disconnection, a celebration of my wholeness, and a gateway to deeper intimacy with myself and others.

Erotic Affirmations Journal
#INMYHEALING

@HealingThe EroticSelf

#INMYHEALING
EROTIC AFFIRMATIONS JOURNAL

I AM EMBODIED

HEALING PRACTICE:
USE THIS AFFIRMATION AS INTENTION IN YOUR PRESENCE PRACTICE TO STAY CONNECT TO YOURSELF.

REFLECTIONS: WHAT IS YOUR RELATIONSHIP TO DEFYING DISCONNECTION?

JOURNAL YOUR REFLECTIONS BELOW.

_____
_____
_____
_____
_____
_____
_____
_____
_____
_____
_____
_____
_____
_____

EMBODIED INTELLIGENCE IS THE INTEGRATION OF YOUR EMOTIONAL, EROTIC, AND SOMATIC INTELLIGENCES.

I am a Lover

To be a lover is to radiate warmth, passion, and tenderness in every connection you create. I embrace my capacity to love deeply and authentically—whether it's in romance, friendship, or self-compassion. As a lover, I give and receive affection with intention, honoring the beauty of shared vulnerability. My erotic energy amplifies the joy of loving and being loved, reminding you that intimacy is a sacred exchange. I am a lover of life, a nurturer of connection, and a guardian of desire. In love, I am both fearless and free.

Erotic Affirmations Journal
#INMYHEALING

@HealingThe EroticSelf

#INMYHEALING
EROTIC AFFIRMATIONS JOURNAL

I AM A LOVER

HEALING PRACTICE:
USE THIS AFFIRMATION AS INTENTION IN YOUR PRESENCE PRACTICE & YOUR ABILITY TO BE AND RECEIVE AFFECTION, WARMTH, AND FRIENDSHIP.

REFLECTIONS: WHAT IS YOUR RELATIONSHIP TO YOUR LOVERSHIP?

JOURNAL YOUR REFLECTIONS BELOW.

_____
_____
_____
_____
_____
_____
_____
_____
_____
_____
_____
_____
_____
_____
_____

BEING A LOVER MEANS YOU ARE WILLING TO GIVE, RECEIVE, AND HONOR YOUR VULNERABILITIES.

I Speak Life into Myself Daily

Speaking life into myself is an erotic act, a declaration that I am worthy of joy, pleasure, and growth. Each word of affirmation becomes a tender caress, awakening my soul to its limitless potential. My thoughts and my voice are well of desire and self-belief, building a foundation of pleasure, love and possibility. As I speak life daily, I embody the truth that I am my most passionate advocate and lover.

Erotic Affirmations Journal
#INMYHEALING

@HealingThe EroticSelf

#INMYHEALING
EROTIC AFFIRMATIONS JOURNAL

I SPEAK LIFE INTO MYSELF DAILY

HEALING PRACTICE:
USE THIS AFFIRMATION AS INTENTION IN YOUR PRESENCE PRACTICE'S INNER DIALOGUE ENCOURAGING YOU TO REMEMBER YOUR POWER AND YOUR PEACE.

REFLECTIONS: WHAT IS YOUR RELATIONSHIP TO ADVOCATING FOR YOURSELF?

JOURNAL YOUR REFLECTIONS BELOW.

_____
_____
_____
_____
_____
_____
_____
_____
_____
_____
_____
_____
_____

"WATCH YOUR THOUGHTS, THEY BECOME YOUR WORDS; WATCH YOUR WORDS, THEY BECOME YOUR ACTIONS; WATCH YOUR ACTIONS, THEY BECOME YOUR HABITS; WATCH YOUR HABITS, THEY BECOME YOUR CHARACTER; WATCH YOUR CHARACTER, IT BECOMES YOUR DESTINY."
— LAO TZU

I am Sexual

I embrace my sexual energy as a natural and vital part of who I am. My sexuality is not defined by societal defaults but by my desired experiences, fantasies, and pleasures. To be sexual is to honor my power to give and receive joy through my body, heart, and mind.

Erotic Affirmations Journal
#INMYHEALING
@HealingThe EroticSelf

#INMYHEALING
EROTIC AFFIRMATIONS JOURNAL

I AM SEXUAL

HEALING PRACTICE:
USE THIS AFFIRMATION AS INTENTION IN YOUR PRESENCE PRACTICE TO CONNECT WITH YOUR SEXUAL SELF.

REFLECTIONS: WHAT IS YOUR RELATIONSHIP TO YOUR SEXUAL SELF?

JOURNAL YOUR REFLECTIONS BELOW.

_____
_____
_____
_____
_____
_____
_____
_____
_____
_____
_____
_____
_____
_____
_____

ASEXUALITY MEANS ONE DOES NOT HAVE THE DESIRE TO HAVE SEXUAL EXPERIENCES. THAT DOES NOT MEAN ONE CAN'T BE SEXUAL.

I am a Creator

My desires are the seeds of my manifestations. My erotic energy is the life force that fuels creation—whether it's in love, art, intimacy, or self-expression. I hold the power to birth new realities, crafting my desires with intention and purpose. Every thought, every action, every breath is an act of creation. As I embrace my erotic energy as a source of creation, I will watch how my passions, dreams, and pleasures come alive in beautiful, transformative ways.

Erotic Affirmations Journal
#INMYHEALING
@HealingThe EroticSelf

#INMYHEALING
EROTIC AFFIRMATIONS JOURNAL

I AM CREATOR

HEALING PRACTICE:
USE THIS AFFIRMATION AS INTENTION IN YOUR PRESENCE PRACTICE TO MANIFEST YOUR DESIRES.

REFLECTIONS: WHAT IS YOUR RELATIONSHIP TO YOUR CREATIVITY?

JOURNAL YOUR REFLECTIONS BELOW.

_____
_____
_____
_____
_____
_____
_____
_____
_____
_____
_____
_____

YOU ARE CREATING SOMETHING IN THIS EVERY MOMENT. BE EXCITED FOR YOURSELF.

I am Aligned

To be aligned is to live in harmony with my true desires and the energy that flows through me because I have learned to surrender to the rhythms of my wholeness, trusting that my erotic energy knows exactly where to lead me. When I am aligned, there is a deep sense of balance between my mind, body, energy, and spirit. I move with ease and confidence, feeling grounded and connected to the infinite flow of pleasure and power. Alignment allows me to embrace my authentic self sincerely and comfortably, allowing my desires to unfold naturally, in perfect harmony with the world around me.

Erotic Affirmations Journal
#INMYHEALING
@HealingTheEroticSelf

#INMYHEALING
EROTIC AFFIRMATIONS JOURNAL

I AM ALIGNED

HEALING PRACTICE:
USE THIS AFFIRMATION AS INTENTION IN YOUR PRESENCE PRACTICE TO YOUR ABILITY TO BE IN HARMONY WITH YOURSELF.

REFLECTIONS: WHAT IS YOUR RELATIONSHIP TO SURRENDER?

JOURNAL YOUR REFLECTIONS BELOW.

_____
_____
_____
_____
_____
_____
_____
_____
_____
_____
_____
_____
_____
_____

THINGS MAY NOT BE CLEAR NOW. THAT IS STILL ALIGHMENT. ALIGHMENT IS NOT ALWAYS AWARENESS. YOUR ENERGY PRACTICES WILL CREATE YOUR ALIGHMENT.

I am Enough

I embrace the fullness of who am I, exactly as I am. I am surrendering my need for the validation of others and instead turn inward to honor my innate worthiness. I am a masterpiece of desires, sensations, and emotions—complete and whole. My erotic energy flourishes when I trust that I am enough to feel, to give, and to receive love and pleasure.

I celebrate my truth with every breath and every touch, knowing that my existence is a profound Divine gift to myself and the world.

Erotic Affirmations Journal
#INMYHEALING
@HealingThe EroticSelf

#INMYHEALING
EROTIC AFFIRMATIONS JOURNAL

I AM ENOUGH

HEALING PRACTICE:
USE THIS AFFIRMATION AS INTENTION IN YOUR PRESENCE PRACTICE KNOWING YOUR SELF-WORTH.

REFLECTIONS: WHAT IS YOUR RELATIONSHIP TO YOUR SELF-WORTH?

JOURNAL YOUR REFLECTIONS BELOW.

_____
_____
_____
_____
_____
_____
_____
_____
_____
_____
_____
_____
_____
_____
_____

BABY STEPS ARE STILL STEPS FORWARD.
-GEORGE T. QUEEN, SR.

#INMYHEALING
EROTIC AFFIRMATIONS JOURNAL

AFFIRMATIONS FOR EACH ENERGY CENTER

These erotic affirmations journal focused on the 1st energy center, the root center. This center is responsible for creating the energy of stability and safety as illustrated in the SHIFT energy chart. Each energy center creates different energy, so each center has a different affirmation. Below are examples of the remaining energy center and their corresponding affirmations. I invite you to create your own erotic affirmation for these centers. You are the answer you seek, the fruit of your emotional labor so let go of perfectionism and create your healing narratives.

2nd Energy Center commonly known as Sacral Chakra (I Feel)
- Theme: Pleasure, creativity, and emotional balance.
- Examples:
  - "I embrace my creativity and passion."
  - "I honor my desires and feelings."
- Erotic Affirmation Activity: How do you honor your desires and creativity? In the space below, create erotic affirmation to deepen this connection:

_____

_____

_____

3rd Energy Center commonly known as Solar Plexus Chakra (I Do)
- Theme: Confidence, power, and action.
- Examples:
  - "I take inspired action toward my goals."
  - "I am strong, capable, and confident."
- Erotic Affirmation Activity: What action are you ready to take? Write an erotic affirmation to empower your steps.

_____

_____

_____

#INMYHEALING
EROTIC AFFIRMATIONS JOURNAL

AFFIRMATIONS FOR EACH ENERGY CENTER

These erotic affirmations journal focused on the 1st energy center, the root center. This center is responsible for creating the energy of stability and safety as illustrated in the SHIFT energy chart. Each energy center creates different energy, so each center has a different affirmation. Below are examples of the remaining energy center and their corresponding affirmations. I invite you to create your own erotic affirmation for these centers. You are the answer you seek, the fruit of your emotional labor so let go of perfectionism and create your healing narratives.

- **4th Energy Center commonly known as Heart Chakra (I Love)**
- Theme: Love, self-compassion, and empathy
- "I give and receive love effortlessly."
- "I am open to love and kindness."
- Erotic Affirmation Activity: Reflect on the love you hold for yourself and others. Create an erotic affirmation that nurtures this energy.

_____

_____

_____

- **5th Energy Center commonly known as Throat Chakra (I Speak)**
- Theme: Communication, truth, and self-expression.
- Examples:
- "I speak my truth with clarity and confidence."
- "My voice is powerful and authentic."
- Erotic Affirmation Activity: What truth do you want to express? Write an erotic affirmation that honors your voice.

_____

_____

_____

#INMYHEALING
EROTIC AFFIRMATIONS JOURNAL

AFFIRMATIONS FOR EACH ENERGY CENTER

These erotic affirmations journal focused on the 1st energy center, the root center. This center is responsible for creating the energy of stability and safety as illustrated in the SHIFT energy chart. Each energy center creates different energy, so each center has a different affirmation. Below are examples of the remaining energy center and their corresponding affirmations. I invite you to create your own erotic affirmation for these centers. You are the answer you seek, the fruit of your emotional labor so let go of perfectionism and create your healing narratives.

6th Energy Center commonly known as Third Eye Chakra (I See)
- Theme: Discernment, knowing oneself, and clarity.
- Examples:
    - "I trust my inner guidance."
    - "I see the path clearly before me."
- Erotic Affirmation Activity: Reflect on how you trust your intuition and create an erotic affirmation that inspires your vision.

_____
_____
_____

7th Energy Center commonly known as Crown Chakra (I Know)
- Theme: Spiritual connection, divine wisdom, and enlightenment.
- Examples:
    - "I trust in the infinite wisdom of the universe."
    - "I am connected to my higher self."
- Erotic Affirmation Activity: How do you connect with your spiritual truth? Write your own affirmation to deepen this bond.

_____
_____
_____

#INMYHEALING
EROTIC AFFIRMATIONS JOURNAL

PRESENCE PRACTICE: CREATING AN EMPOWERED EMBODIMENT

Developing Your Presence Practice

You have to be present for the relationships you want, both with self and in community with others. This presence practice is not only the skill of holding space, but also the alchemy of your lovership and kinship for both your personal and professional relationships.

As a trauma-informed licensed social work and therapist, I often use the analogy that healing is the feeling one has when they are healing from a paper cut . It is itchy, uncomfortable, and sometimes painful, however, instead of scratching and reopening the wound, you manage the uncomfortableness by soothing both yourself and that wound. This is what I witness my clients achieve when they focus on the pleasure-affirming healing relationship with their mind, body energy, and spirit and not just on their therapy and coaching outcomes.

Our relationship to our mind, body, energy, and spirit is informed by our lived experience and our ability to access embodied safety and self-trust. Our lived experience also informs our perception of self. Your wounds make you feel chaotic. Being able to manage the distress and/or discomfort of our wounds by establishing embodied safety and developing self-trust, in ancestral medicine, this healing process is called shadow work; and in neuroscience, specifically neuroplasticity, this healing process is called the Polyvagal Theory, and integrative somatic understanding, this healing process is what I call "self-liberation." Self-liberation is a practice, a skill, and an embodiment.

#INMYHEALING
EROTIC AFFIRMATIONS JOURNAL

PRESENCE PRACTICE: CREATING AN EMPOWERED EMBODIMENT

To liberate yourself in your personal healing and even your professional development. you will learn to intentionally disrupt, challenge, deconstruct, decenter, unpack, and unlearn societal and sexual assumptions and expectations. This is the practice of decolonization.

To become present with embodied safety and self-trust that challenges "the defaults" of societal and sexual assumptions and expectations, have you considered decolonization as a care practice?

As a self-liberator and space holder, I can tell you decolonization is the healing practice, process, and framework of self and collective liberation.

However- You can't only feel good, avoid, self-sacrifice, disassociate, or distract your way to liberation.

To liberate yourself, you can't bypass shadow work.
Shadow work is how you heal.
The erotic will decolonize your healing.
Sexual shadow work is how you become self-liberated.

This is decolonial somatic healing. Decolonial somatic healing is the understanding, disruption, unlearning, and liberation from the relationship between oppression and its impact on a marginalized person's mind, body, energy, and spirit.

#INMYHEALING
EROTIC AFFIRMATIONS JOURNAL

PRESENCE PRACTICE: CREATING AN EMPOWERED EMBODIMENT

With your permission, allow me to remind you: You are a lover and you are already WHOLE. Regardless of "the defaults" of and harmed caused by societal and sexual expectations and assumptions, our purpose in life is to "live WHOLE pleasurably ". Unfortunately, these defaults and trauma we experience disrupts the connection to our wholeness and to pleasure. According to neuroscience, it takes 66 days of a practice to become embodied, part of who you are.
When creating embodied safety and trust with relationships, either with ourselves or with our loved ones, we need to be in relationship with our ability to be discerning via capacity, capability, and desirability.

The components of discernment are:

1. Capacity is our mental and emotional space to be present.
2. Capability is our ability to receive and process what's communicated.
3. Desirability is not only being wanted, it is what one wants.

In order to create such an embodiment, I am encouraging you to develop a presence practice you can do with ease and effort with system of self-care and healing routines you can practice daily, weekly, monthly, and yearly.

What do I mean by presence practice?

#INMYHEALING
EROTIC AFFIRMATIONS JOURNAL

PRESENCE PRACTICE: CREATING AN EMPOWERED EMBODIMENT

Your presence practice is:

1. **Awareness:**
   Your conscious and subconscious ability to receive and process information through your five senses and your intuition, your 6th sense.
2. **Intention:**
   A deliberate purpose of the current moment, activity, or event you are in.
3. **Effort:**
   The commitment of intentional action through the movement of your mindset (decision-making process), moods, and movements (behaviors).

With self-compassion and curiosity within your day-to-day interactions, #InMyHealing Erotic Affirmations will help you create an empowering mindset to challenge automatic negative thinking and self-doubt and using SHIFT, A Self-Liberation Practice, you will overcome the "fuck-its" of self-sacrificing behaviors and improve your ability to manage distressing emotions by helping you create self-regulated boundaries and reduce impulsive decision-making.

Together #InMyHealing Erotic Affirmations, SHIFT, A Self-Liberation Practice, and the workbook for sexual shadow work, Healing The Erotic Self, will help you decolonize the healing of your moods, mindset, and movement so you can decolonize your healing for empowered ways of developing and sustaining intimacy within your relationships with Self and your loved ones.

#INMYHEALING
EROTIC AFFIRMATIONS JOURNAL

SHIFT, A SELF-LIBERATION PRACTICE
DEVELOPING AN EMBODIED PRESENCE CARE PRACTICE

Instructions: Follow the directions of each care practice. Use together or individually based on the level of care you need.

1. *Ground:*

Grounding is a self-awareness, conscious presence, the practice of being present to one's distress, safety, and/or discomfort and to what intensity.

a. Take 3 full belly breaths at the count of 4-4-4 (inhale-hold-exhale)
b. Scale intensity from 0 (not intense) to 10 (very intense) the sexual distress or sexual discomfort you are experiencing.
c. Where in your body to you feel safe or not safe? Note it. This will be helpful in the next practices.
d. Use Your Presence Practice of Your Awareness + Your Intention + Your Effort.
Stay present in the moment. This will combat disassociation or other trauma responses.

2. Center:

Centering is a *self-soothing, self-compassion, self-guidance practice via asking clarifying questions. Self-soothing is the practice of taking care of one's emotions in the present moment. Ask yourself:*
a. Who are you centering?
b. What is the purpose of this moment?
c. What is/are the self-witnessed emotion(s) telling me about myself and sense of safety?

3. *Nurture:*

Nurturing is a *self-regulation, self-preservation, practice informed by one's relationship to their senses, energy, and spirit; the conscious awareness of one's energy.*
a. What care practices can I do to take care of myself: List 5 self-soothing activities that engage your senses (touch, hear, etc.) to practice from 10-15 minutes. This will help you create safety from within and support you, mind, body and/or energy, by decreasing the intensity of your witnessed distress and/or discomfort. The practice engages your nervous system which regulates your response to distress.

4. *Affirm:*

Affirmation-- a mindfulness, self-assuring, self-talk practice used to disrupt and dissolve intrusive thinking and automatic negative thoughts with empowering beliefs; can be used in nurturing practices.
Using the empowering beliefs and the seven (7) uses the erotic shared earlier, create erotic affirmation to support and as part of your nurturing practice.
Example: I am desirable. For more support with erotic affirmations, get the erotic affirmations journal, #InMyHealing.

HEALING THE EROTIC SELF
The SHIFT Energy Center Chart

Gland		Energy Center
ACCESS TO QUANTUM FIELD MEMORY — The KA		**8TH ENERGY CENTER** — CONNECTION TO THE COSMOS, EPIPHANIES, DOWNLOADS
PINEAL GLAND — DOOR TO HIGHER CONSCIOUSNESS		**CROWN	7TH ENERGY CENTER** — SELF AS SOURCE, SELF-ASSURED, DIVINITY
PITUITARY GLAND — DOOR TO INNER SELF-CONSCIOUSNESS		**THIRD EYE	6TH ENERGY CENTER** — SELF-AWARENESS, SELF-ESTEEM, & DISCERNMENT
THYROID GLAND — METABOLISM		**THROAT	5TH ENERGY CENTER** — TRUTH AND COMMUNICATION
THYMUS GLAND — EXPANSION, REPAIR, REGENERATION		**HEART	4TH ENERGY CENTER** — LOVE, SELF-COMPASSION, HOPE, OPTIMISM
PANCREAS & DIGESTIVE GLANDS — STRESS, DIGESTION, CONSUMPTION, PROCESSING, AND RELEASE		**SOLAR PLEXUS	3RD ENERGY CENTER** — CONNECTION, SELF-CONFIDENCE, INTUITION "GUT FEELING"
ARENDALS & REPRODUCTIVE GLANDS — LONGING, DIGESTION, CONSUMPTION, PROCESSING, AND RELEASE		**SACRAL	2ND ENERGY CENTER** — CREATIVITY & DESIRABILITY, SELF-WORTH
REPRODUCTIVE GLANDS — SAFETY, SEXUALITY, & ELIMINATION		**ROOT ENERGY	1ST ENERGY CENTER** — SAFETY, SECURITY, & STABILITY

The SHIFT Energy Chart
Ancestral knowing confirmed by the neuroscience and neuroplasticity

Identify your healing themes
&
what informs your healing practices

SHIFT, A Self-Liberation Healing Practice
Mx. Lena Queen, LCSW, M.Ed.
(c) copyright 2023

ENERGY CENTERS & ENDOCRINE SYSTEM

SHIFT, A Self-Liberation Healing Practice Care Plan

_____

I. Ground: Establish Safety and Stay Present

1. Take 3 FULL Breaths
2. Core Wounds: (Self-Worth, Self-Esteem, Self-Confidence)
    a. What's the Witnessed
        Emoton(s):_____

3. Where do you feel it in your body: _____

4. What age do you feel: _____

II. Center: Get Clear & Create Your Intentions

1. Process SHIFT's Clarifying Questions (See Book)

2. Name Your Self-Limitng Beliefs:
    _____

3. Healing Theme (Energy Center-See SHIFT Energy Chart):
    _____

4. Shadow Work (Self-Sabotaging Behavior to Address):
    _____

III. Nurture: Your Care Practices to Establish Safety & Develop an Intuitive Self-Trust

1. Mind (Meditation):
    _____

2. Body (Mindful Movement):
    _____

3. Spirit (Energy Practice):
    _____

IV. Affirm: Create an Empowering Belief of Your Self

1. My Erotic Affirmation: _____

Self-Reflection: SHIFT Integration Practice

Who are you without the impact of that core wound? Who are you in your healing?

#INMYHEALING
EROTIC AFFIRMATIONS JOURNAL

WITNESSING: EMBRACING SELF-ACCOUNTABILITY

Be a Witness: Observe Your Embodiment

SHIFT is not just a somatic healing practice and system of self-care. SHIFT is an embodied wellness practice honoring the intuitive relationship of the mind, body, energy, and spirit--a practice of self-permission, self-compassion, and self-trust. Our embodiment is a reflection of our beliefs, our mindsets, and our energy. To witness means to observe compassionately and without judgment of one's embodiment. So many times as a coach and therapist, I am educating clients and mentees to see their embodiment as reflections of their sense of Self, not just as causes of trauma, self-sabotaging beliefs, mindsets, behaviors, and energy. There comes a time when you will need to explore your habits or the patterns of behavior that no longer serve you, and the mindsets and energy that inform them. Trauma responses may have protected you in the past and that is important to honor. Now, you are in a place of healing where you must examine the mindsets, habits, and actions that hinder your ability to trust yourself and connect to your Self in ways that is intuitive and self-trusting. You will become empowered in your healing journey to identify care practices and healing strategies in ways of being that align with your most authentic self. By consciously releasing self-sabotaging beliefs, mindsets, and behaviors, you create space for healing transformation and the emergence of your true and WHOLE-Self.

Ownership: Becoming the Author of Your Life

Ownership is just that- your intentional connection and self-accountability to your mindset, your behaviors, and your embodiment. Ownership is the key that unlocks our potential for healing our core wounds. In this workbook, you have explored the profound act of embracing ownership over your sexual distress, sexual pleasure, sexual experiences, and sexual emotions. By acknowledging that you are the author of your life, you reclaim the ability to make decisions and develop self-trust, power, and confidence over the perception of your lived experience, sexually and non-sexually. You shed the role of passive spectating and step into the role of an empowered creator, shaping your healing narratives with intention, authenticity, pleasure, and purpose. I encourage you to use the reflection notes of this healing guide to journal intentionally about your takeaways and self-reflections- to unpack what you have discovered about yourself, your healing values, and your erotic self.

#INMYHEALING
EROTIC AFFIRMATIONS JOURNAL
BODY SCAN:
A GROUNDING AND SELF-AWARENESS PRACTICE

Directions: On your phone's voice memo, record yourself using the directions below and use as the nuture practice to SHIFT.

- Sit or lie down comfortably, and gently close your eyes.
- Begin by taking a deep breath in through your nose, filling your lungs, and exhale slowly through your mouth, releasing any tension.
- Shift your focus to your toes. Feel any sensations there—warmth, tingling, or relaxation. Take a breath and allow them to soften.
- Move your attention upward to your feet, heels, and ankles. Notice any tension or points of contact with the ground. Breathe into these areas, letting go of any stress.
- Shift your awareness to your calves and knees. Feel the muscles relaxing with each breath, releasing any tightness.
- Move up to your thighs and hips. Sense the weight of your body being supported. Breathe deeply and let any remaining tension melt away.
- Shift your focus to your lower back, abdomen, and chest. Notice the gentle rise and fall of your breath. Allow these areas to loosen and relax further.
- Bring your attention to your hands. Feel the sensations in your fingers, palms, and wrists. Breathe out any tension, letting it dissipate.
- Move up to your forearms, elbows, and upper arms. Notice any sensations or areas of tightness. With each breath, let go of any remaining stress.
- Shift your awareness to your shoulders. Release any tension you might be holding there. Breathe into this space, allowing your shoulders to soften and drop.
- Now, focus on your neck, throat, and jaw. Let these muscles relax. Take a moment to release any tightness with your breath.
- Finally, direct your attention to your head and face. Soften your forehead, relax your jaw, and ease any tension around your eyes.
- Take a moment to scan your entire body, feeling a sense of relaxation and grounding.
- Slowly bring your attention back to your breath. Take a few deep breaths, feeling the calmness and steadiness of each inhale and exhale.
- When you're ready, gently open your eyes. Take a moment to notice how your body feels—relaxed, grounded, and present.

#INMYHEALING
EROTIC AFFIRMATIONS JOURNAL

PLEASURE ACTIVISM

RESOURCES

Whether you are familiar with pleasure activism or this is your first time exploring pleasure activism, below is a small list of pleasure activists, I encourage you to become familiar with their work as a resource for your own self-pleasure activism, healing, and self-liberation:

- Audre Lorde: Uses of the Erotic and Sister Outsider
- Adrienne Marie Brown Pleasure-Activism
- bell hooks: All About Love and everything she has written
- Tracy Q. Gilbert, Ph.D., Emotional IQ Coach, The Erotic Self creator and author of Black & Sexy: A Framework of Black Sexuality in the 21st Century
- Jenaee Hopgood, LMFT & BlackAngelMom.com
- Lyvonne Brigg's Sensual Faith
- Dr. Donna Oriowo & her Cocoabutter & Hairgrease Workbook
- Dr. Lexx's Black Girls Guide to Couple's Intimacy
- Afrosexology & their course and workbooks
- The Ultimate Guide to Seduction by Marla Renee Steward & Dr. Jessica O'Reilly
- Tracy Rose, Ph.D.'s Longing to Tell
- Staci Haines' Healing Sex: A MindBody Approach to Healing Sexual Trauma
- Zelaika Hepworth-Clarke, Ph.D. Flow of Oshunality Model
- Amina Peterson's Authentic Consent
- Roger Kuhn's SomaCultural Liberation
- Black Girl Bliss Books
- Spiritual Books by Monique Joiner Seidlak
- Chanta Blue, LCSW, CST (IG: @NJSexTherapist)
- Bryon Russell, Men's Mental Health and Sexuality (IG: @CounselorCharli)
- BlackGirlsGuidetoSurvivingMenopause.com
- Healing The Erotic Self-Life Coaching Program on Patreon
- SHIFT, A Self-Liberation Healing Practice Quick Guide
- Erotic Intelligence: The Other EQ Masterclass

Self-Reflections

Self-Reflections

Self-Reflections

Decolonizing Healing & Healing The Erotic Self

Integrative Somatic Healing

Healing The Erotic Self Workbook & Coaching

Sexuality & Somatics Professional Development & Learning Series

SHIFT Somatic Healing Practice & Coaching

DISCOVER MORE ABOUT MX. LENA QUEEN, LCSW, M.ED (QUEEN/THEY)

Website: SistaSexologist.com

Connect with Me

 @SistaSexologist

 @MxLenaQueen

 @SistaSexologist

 Healing The Erotic Self

More about Queen

With over 22 years of both personal and professional healing, public speaking, training, and writing experience, Clinical Somatic Sexologist, Embodied Wellness, and Erotic Coach, Mx. Queen offers an integrative, pleasure-affirming, and healing-centered approach to somatic sexology, life coaching, corporate wellness, and healing entrepreneurship. Their offerings include their integrative somatic psychotherapy & Integrative Somatic Sex Therapy & Approach (I-SST) practice, Journey Wellness & Consulting; their teaching and consultation non-profit, The WHOLE-Self Healing Institute, Inc. signature life coaching program, Healing The Erotic Self, in addition to, sexual wellness and erotic liberation retreat, Healing Your Erotic Energy, and masterclass, The Other EQ: Erotic Intelligence. Queen is also the author of the workbook for sexual shadow work, Healing The Erotic Self and the integrative somatic healing ebook, SHIFT, A Self-Liberation Healing Practice Quick Guide.

Queen, a Black queer person, is a TEDx Speaker and author, kink-aware professional, speaker, lecturer, and adjunct professor who has contributed to articles and media interviews regarding sexuality & post-traumatic growth and healing.

Continue your journey towards sexual healing and sexual liberation with Healing The Erotic Self, A Workbook for Sexual Shadow Workbook.

LET'S CURATE HEALING SPACES TOGETHER.

www.ingramcontent.com/pod-product-compliance
Lightning Source LLC
Chambersburg PA
CBHW051512100526
44585CB00043B/2470